Why Do We Have to Be So Quiet in Church?

And **12** Other Questions Kids Have About God

Clare Simpson
Illustrated by Kay Harker

PARACLETE PRESS
Brewster, Massachusetts

2013 First Printing
Why Do We Have to Be So Quiet in Church? And 12 Other Questions Kids Have About God
Copyright © 2013 by Paraclete Press, Inc.

ISBN: 978-1-61261-371-0

Scriptural references marked NRSV are taken from the New Revised Standard Version of the Bible, copyright 1989, 1995 by the Division of Christian Education of the National Council of Churches of Christ in the United States of America and are used by permission. All rights reserved.

Scriptural references marked NIV are taken from The Holy Bible, New International Version®, NIV® Copyright © 1973, 1978, 1984, 2011 by Biblica, Inc. Used by permission. All rights reserved worldwide.

Scripture references marked KJV are taken from the King James Version of the Holy Bible.

Scripture references marked ESV are taken from The Holy Bible, English Standard Version, copyright © 2001 by Crossway Bibles, a division of Good News Publishers. Used by permission. All rights reserved.

Scripture references marked GNT are taken from the Good News Translation—Second Edition. Copyright © 1992 by American Bible Society. Used by permission. All rights reserved.

Sources:
p. 10: "Make a joyful noise to the LORD." Psalm 100:1 (ESV)
p. 12: He even knows how many hairs are on our heads! See Luke 12:7.
p. 16: "Come, let us bow down in worship, let us kneel before the LORD our Maker." Psalm 95:6 (NIV)
p. 18: "God is spirit." John 4:24; "God is love." 1 John 4:8 (NRSV)
p. 20: "Morning, noon, and night my complaints and groans go up to him, and he will hear my voice." Psalm 55:17 (GNT)
p. 22: See Psalm 139:7–10.
p. 24: See Romans 8:14–17 and Galatians 3:26–28.
p. 28: See Hebrews 8:12.
p. 30: "We love him, because he first loved us." 1 John 4:19 (KJV)

Library of Congress Cataloging-in-Publication Data
Simpson, Clare.
  Why do we have to be so quiet in church? : and 12 other questions kids have about God / Clare Simpson.
    pages cm
  ISBN 978-1-61261-371-0
  1. Church—Juvenile literature. 2. God (Christianity)—Juvenile literature. I. Title.
  BV602.5.S56 2013
  264.0083—dc23   2013000989

The Paraclete Press name and logo (dove on cross) is a registered trademark of Paraclete Press, Inc.

10 9 8 7 6 5 4 3 2 1

Published by Paraclete Press, Brewster, Massachusetts, www.paracletepress.com

Printed in China

This book belongs to

_____

4

I love going to church with my family.
My mom and dad sit beside me.
We sing.
We pray.
We listen to stories from the Bible.

But why do we have to be so quiet in church?

It's good to be quiet and listen,
and I know the people around me
want to listen too.

I have friends at church.
I see them every week.

Does God like it when we play together?

Jesus played when he was a child,
and he loved to watch children play
when he was grown up.

I love to sing hymns and songs.
My friends love to sing too.
But sometimes we sing and talk too loud
in church. Our teacher tells us we should
quiet down.

Does God hear me when I sing?

"Make a joyful noise to the LORD," the Bible says!

I try to listen when I'm in church.
It can be hard to listen.
It can be hard to sit still.
But I try.
Sometimes, Mom tells me I did a great
job of sitting still and listening.

Can God see me in church?

God always sees you.
He even knows how many hairs are
on your head!

In church, we often say the same things over and over. We talk about God, and Jesus, the Bible, and Baptism, and about how we need to have faith like children. I like that part.

Why do we say "Amen" at the end of everything?

"Amen" is our simple way of saying:
I agree!

I once heard the word *reverent*.
It means to be respectful and to worship.
I try to be reverent toward God.
I come to church to worship him.

Does God like it when I kneel or bow my head?

King David wrote in the Psalms:
"Come, let us bow down
in worship,
let us kneel before the LORD."

I don't always understand what is happening in church. So sometimes I sit and think about other things. Dad says it's okay to think about other things sometimes.

What does God look like?

**God is spirit. God is love.
God looks different from anything
you can imagine.**

Sometimes when I think,
I also say little prayers quietly,
inside my own head.

Can God always hear me?

Oh yes, the Bible says God hears us morning, noon, and night—in other words, always!

We stand up and sit down a lot in church.
We kneel.
I like it when we get to move,
because I start wiggling when
I have to sit still too long!

Can God see me, no matter where I go,
or what I do?

We can never wander away
from God. God is everywhere.

Babies get baptized in our church.

I love to watch.

Mom tells me she remembers my Baptism.

"Do *you* remember?" she asks me.

But of course I don't remember—

I was only a baby!

Does God remember my Baptism?

Of course, he does, because Baptism is when God seals us as his very own.

We always ask for forgiveness in church.
God, please forgive me.
Forgive me for pouting. Forgive me for talking angrily to my mom. Forgive me for pushing my brother.

Does God see me when I do something wrong?

God sees everything, everywhere.

Doing something wrong is called "sin."
I learned that in church.
I do wrong things sometimes. But I
learned in church that God loves sinners.
I'm glad he loves me.

Does God really forgive my sins?

More than that, the Bible says
God loves us so much
that he forgets them too, as if we
never did anything wrong.

I love the stories in the Bible
about Jesus most of all.
Jesus was like a shepherd with lots of
sheep, caring for every single one of them.

I love how Jesus cares for me!

"We love him
because he first loved us,"
the Bible says.

When we're leaving church, I see all my friends and I know they like me and care about me. The people in church feel like my aunts and uncles, friends and cousins.

God, did you make church
just for me?
I think you did. Thank you.
Wait . . . I mean,
Amen!